LIFE IN
The 1960s

Mike Brown

The Home

The lean years of the 40s and early 50s had given way to a boom; employment was high, as were incomes – after years of austerity, people wanted a change. The latest architectural style was Modernism, based on rigid geometric shapes made using concrete cast in situ. The results were often stark, leading to the alternate name 'Brutalist'. Examples include Birmingham's Bull Ring (1964), London's Elephant and Castle shopping centre (1965), and the Hayward Gallery (1968). Most representative of the period, however, are tower blocks, which were considered the solution to the housing shortage and began to spring up in every city.

House prices were rising. The average house price in 1960 was £2,500 (2.7 times the average annual wage), and this almost doubled to £4,600 by 1969 (2.9 times). By 1961, the average married couple owned a television set and a vacuum cleaner and most had a washing machine and fridge. By 1960, a fifth had a freezer and by 1965, a half.

People also did their own decorating. To help with this, the 1962 BBC TV series *Bucknell's House* followed DIY guru Barry Bucknell as he

◄ Elvis Presley at his Graceland home, 1965.

◄ The Bull Ring shopping centre in the heart of Birmingham, 1966.

furniture matched with Art Deco figurines, Edwardian prints and quirky items picked up from a junk market.

Furniture tended towards the futuristic: the inflatable 'blow' armchair was a great hit, but in an age where most people smoked, punctures were a real danger. Moulded plastic was more solid, such as the Finnish Ball/Globe chair, or the 'pastilli' – like a beanbag but solid. Indeed, the beanbag chair, originally called *il sacco*, was designed by an Italian company in 1969. Even

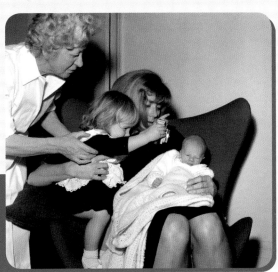

► Actress Vanessa Redgrave, with daughters Natasha Richardson and Joely Richardson, sits in an Egg Chair, 1965.

renovated a house over 39 weeks. Domestic design in the second half of the 60s tended to be quirky. Themes either related to the hyper-modern – such as a TV set based on an astronaut's helmet, or a room heater which looked like a flying saucer – or looked back at late Victorian/Edwardian styles: pictures of Lord Kitchener or Dr Livingstone, or period advertising, either original or printed on tins, trays or aprons. Wallpaper tended to be in bold, slightly muddy, pastel colours such as orange, green and brown. Designs were geometric, 'op-art' (giving the effect of an optical illusion), psychedelic paisley-type effects, or simple cartoon-like shapes, often in primary or pastel colours. The overall look sought was eclectic, with pieces of modernistic

traditional leather armchairs were updated, such as the Egg Chair, by Arne Jacobson. Perhaps most iconic were the various hanging chairs, based on the ball, egg or globe shape, but suspended from the ceiling or from a frame.

Fashionable crockery, including Poole and Troika, had a handmade feel. The basic shapes were simple, often cylindrical; background colours were white offset by a lid or cup in a bold primary colour, or pastel with stylised designs in the form of cartoon-like flowers, leaves or fruit. Glassware was heavy and chunky, such as Whitefriars, again often in orange, green, blue or brown. Drinking glasses tended to be of the tumbler-type, clear, with a simple repeat design.

Working Lives

Employment was high: unemployment averaged around 2 per cent, never going above 2.6 per cent. The type of work people did was changing rapidly. In manufacturing, Britain lost a quarter of a million jobs over the decade. By 1960, the Lancashire cotton industry, previously a huge employer, was dead, killed by a combination of lack of investment and cheap overseas labour. That year Britain was the world's second largest motor vehicle producer, but within six years Britain had slipped to fourth. However, by the end of the decade manufacturing still made up 30 per cent of Britain's Gross Domestic Product (GDP), as opposed to 12 per cent in 2010.

Although there were just under a quarter of a million apprentices in 1965, there were growing concerns about the scheme, which was criticised, like much of industry, for being male-dominated, outdated, and failing to embrace new and expanding occupations. Such technological developments had

▲ A computer from the 1960s, used for translations.

◄ Copytakers at work in Fleet Street, London, 1967.

◀ London Bridge with the docklands behind it seen from Southwark Bank, 1965.

The average man's salary rose from a little under £1,000 a year in 1960 to £1,600 in 1969, highlighting the high rate of inflation over the decade. For women, average salaries were roughly only half that of their male counterparts, and they were far more likely to be in unskilled jobs. Two-thirds were classed as non-manual, like clerks, typists and shop assistants. Only about 5 per cent of managers were women; in some industries the proportion was as low as 1 per cent. But this was not being meekly accepted: in what has been called the second wave of feminism, the status quo was being challenged.

Commonwealth citizens were not subject to immigration control until 1962, when tension led to restrictions. Then they were admitted at the rate of about 75,000 per year, which was counterbalanced by emigration. Prejudice created flashpoints, as in Bristol in 1963. A bus company refused to employ black or Asian bus crews, which lead to a boycott of the company's buses by Bristolians and lasted for four months until the company backed down. Two years later, the Race Relations Act outlawed discrimination in public places, while the 1968 Act extended this to employment and housing.

resulted in 1960 in the invention of lasers, while in 1964 the computer language BASIC was invented. In 1967 the first handheld calculator appeared, followed in 1968 by the computer mouse and RAM, and by 1969 the Arpanet, a precursor of the internet, had been created.

Service industry jobs, on the other hand, rose by over 1 million throughout the 60s, although this net gain was not spread evenly. One of the biggest problems for the capital was the demise of docklands. 'Containerisation' was making previous docking practices redundant, and plans were made to shift London's docks to Tilbury. In 1969, St Katharine's became the first of the old docks to close. It became a symbol of the changes, as like the rest of the capital it turned to tourism, the London Tourist Board being set up in 1963.

Average working hours were from 42 to 46 per week. Smoking at work was the norm – in offices or workshops. Seventy per cent of men and 40 per cent of women smoked.

➤ The feminist Betty Friedan, 1966.

Supermarkets were appearing everywhere, and growing in size. In 1960 Tesco opened its Cheltenham store with the then huge floor space of almost 400 square metres. By the late 60s they coined the name 'superstore' for their latest store, which was ten times as big. This growth was partly due to the Resale Prices Act (1964). Before this, retailers could only sell a product at the price determined by the manufacturer, but this was now banned. Large supermarkets were now able to 'Pile 'em high and sell 'em cheap', encouraging customers to use their stores, and creating large national chains.

Another great change was the type of food bought. By the beginning of the 60s, the majority of houses had a refrigerator and a fifth even had a freezer. For them the old habit of the daily shop was a thing of the past, as food could be stored. This was helped by the rapid expansion of frozen food, as companies such as Birds Eye, Findus

and Ross produced new products. By 1965 the proportion of homes with a freezer had risen to a half. In 1968 Bejam stores began to open which only sold frozen foods.

Supermarket competition was huge, and many stores chose to give out gift stamps. Every purchase would entitle you to that amount's worth of stamps, which were licked and stuck into books. These stamps could then be exchanged for gifts from a catalogue. A month's shop might produce many pages of stamps – many will still be able to recall the taste! Gift stamp schemes included Pink Stamps, Co-op dividend stamps, S&H Pink Stamps, and the biggest of all, Green Shield Stamps.

◄ Buildings and shops in Chester, 1960.

◄ Fresh fruit and vegetables on sale at a supermarket in Hounslow, 1963.

▲ TV cookery experts Fanny and Johnny Craddock with a suckling pig, 1960.

▼ Spanish oranges at a Staines supermarket, 1963.

freshest and juiciest!

ESPAÑA

The package tour was booming: one of the first charter airlines, Euravia, commenced flights from Manchester Airport in 1961 and Luton in 1962. Foreign holidays introduced people to new foods, such as spaghetti bolognese. Also, the growth of air travel meant fruit and vegetables could be flown in at any time of the year, and unusual items such as avocados began to appear.

Wine was another thing many first experienced abroad. The consumption of wine doubled over the decade; popular brands included Mateus Rosé, Piat d'Or, Black Tower and Blue Nun. Here, too, the supermarkets could help. In 1962 legislation opened the Off Licence trade to supermarkets, and wine, or a few beers, would be part of the weekly shop. In 1960 almost 40 per cent of beer was sold in bottles – 60 per cent in the south of England. There were cans of beer, but these had to be opened with a tin opener, until 1963 saw the introduction of the ring pull.

Fanny and Johnny Craddock showed the nation how to cook new things. The dinner party was the high point of entertaining; particular party favourites included cheese and pineapple on cocktail sticks, angels and devils on horseback, cheese straws, cocktail sausages and scotch eggs. Even potato crisps became adventurous with new flavours introduced: cheese and onion (1962), smokey bacon (1964), roast chicken (1967), and beef and onion (1969). And all rounded off with After Eight mints (1962).

Relationships

The dance hall, where many couples had met in the 50s, remained popular, but with the growth of pop they had largely become the haunt of the young. Older singles needed to look elsewhere, with potential partners meeting through work romances, blind dates arranged by friends, or at clubs and societies.

During the 1950s, pubs had been a largely male world; their dowdy, smoky atmospheres had not appealed to women. Indeed, 'gents only' bars were still not uncommon in the 60s, especially in the north. This had led to young men deserting them to look for female company elsewhere, such as in coffee bars. The brewers responded by changing the face of pubs. Instead of several small, dark

⌃ The licensee pours a drink at the Hatchet Inn, Sherfield, 1964.

⌃ A couple slow dancing at Hammersmith Palais, 1960.

▲ Renowned birth control pioneer Margaret Sanger in 1961.

▲ Princess Margaret's wedding cake, 1960.

bars, they became open plan, with modern plastic tables and barstools. Drinks changed, too: hand-pulled bitter lost its attraction as pale or light ale, often bottled, rose in popularity. Among younger drinkers, lager with lime squash was an exotic treat. For women, Babycham (sometimes with brandy), gin or vodka and lime, a Snowball or even a glass of wine were the fashion.

In 1961 the 'pill' arrived, bringing deep changes in society. Previously, family planning had been rather hit and miss, and chiefly the responsibility of the man. At first, it was only prescribed to married women – mostly older women who had already had children and wanted no more. But this changed. In the past most women had married at an early age, being expected to give up their job and become a full-time housewife and mother while their husband went out to work. If a woman wanted to follow a career, she had to give up thoughts of marriage. Now, married women could, if they chose, plan a career, and the rigid gender-based division of roles began to change. It was the beginning of both a social and sexual revolution, and there was much talk of 'the permissive society' and 'free love'.

Despite predictions that the pill meant the end of matrimony, marriage rates grew over the 60s, from 344,000 in 1960 to 397,000 in 1969. Yet divorces more than doubled, from 24,000 in 1960 to 51,000 in 1969. The statistics do, however, reflect a loosening of the law. In 1969 the Divorce Reform Act was passed. This allowed couples to divorce after two years of separation if uncontested, and five years otherwise, and neither partner had to prove 'fault'.

In spite of the pill, increasing prosperity brought a higher birth rate: 790,000 babies in 1960 rose to 820,000 by the end of the decade. Most surprising under the circumstances, however, were the illegitimacy figures, from 43,000 to 70,000.

The 1960s were not only permissive towards heterosexuals. In July 1967 Parliament passed the Sexual Offences Act. This decriminalised homosexual acts carried out in private between two men, both over the age of 21. It did not cover the Merchant Navy or the Armed Forces, or apply to Scotland or Northern Ireland. Women were not covered by the act, as sex between women was not a criminal act.

New plastics were a boon to toymakers, and there was a wave of new products. In 1960 the Etch-a-Sketch arrived, followed in 1961 by Scalextric and in 1962 by Mousetrap. Barbie had been launched by the US company Mattel Inc. in March 1959, but in 1963 Pedigree Dolls introduced her British cousin, Sindy, who with her Carnaby Street-style fashions, including a Mary Quant bob, became the best-selling toy in the UK in 1968.

In 1964 it was the boys' turn and Hasbro launched its GI Joe action figure in the US. Palitoy followed in 1966 with Action Man – a licensed copy of GI Joe. There was a negative reaction from those who saw them as 'dolls for boys', but most boys loved them. With 1965 came the Spirograph, and 1967 brought KerPlunk. Then in 1969 came a real icon, the space hopper, which became a craze, as did the Chopper bike.

Pocket money was often spent on chocolate bars, and there were many new ones in the 60s, including Galaxy (1960), Topic (1962), Toffee Crisp (1963) and Twix (1967).

The 60s introduced a host of classic children's television programmes. *Noggin the Nog* first started in 1959 but remained popular until 1965. In 1960 and 1961 US cartoons *The Flintstones*

▲ Homemaker Barbie, from the early 1960s.

and *Topcat* arrived. The following year it was the turn of *Animal Magic*, with the many voices of Johnny Morris. The year 1964 introduced *The Addams Family* and the wonderful world of *The Magic Roundabout*. A year later came the sci-fi options, in the form of *Lost in Space* and *Thunderbirds*; 1966 brought *Batman* (*Kapow!*), the *Clangers*, and possibly the first boyband, The Monkees, who formed as an imitation of the Beatles for the US programme of the same name.

In 1967 *Trumpton* appeared for the first time, as did *Spiderman*. Then in 1968 ITV first broadcast *Magpie*, as a 'hip' rival to *Blue Peter*, which was now ten years old and beginning to look old fashioned. The decade ended with *The Pink Panther Show*, a cartoon based on a character only seen in the credits for the films *The Perils of Penelope Pitstop* and the wonderful *Sesame Street*.

◄ Playtime in south London, 1961.

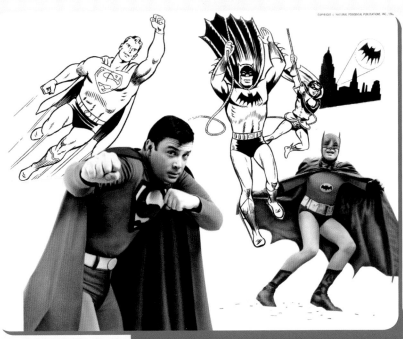

In the early 60s children took an exam called the eleven-plus in their last year of primary school and most were sent to one of two types of school depending on their results. Those who passed went to a grammar school, while the rest, about two-thirds, went to a secondary modern. Those at the grammar were expected to go on

▲ The original Superman cartoon character, with Bob Holiday who plays him, and the original Batman with his Boy Wonder Robin, with actor Adam West in front, 1966.

to university and then join a profession, whereas their counterparts at the secondary modern were expected to go into trades and industry.

Many disapproved of a system that 'failed' most of its children. In the 1964 General Election, Labour promised that it would 'get rid of the segregation of children caused by eleven-plus selection', replacing both types of school with 'comprehensives'. They won, and in 1965 there followed a massive expansion of comprehensive schools across England and Wales. Soon there were less than 200 selective grammar schools remaining.

◀ Puppeteers Christine Glanville and Mary Turner with some of the cast of *Thunderbirds* at the Associated Press Films studio at Slough, 1965.

Teenagers

Since 1949, healthy males between 17 and 21 years old had been expected to do National Service; that is, called up to serve in the Armed Forces for 18 months and remain on the reserve list for four years, during which time they could be recalled three times for up to 20 days. In December 1960 National Service ceased; in November that year the last men were called up, and the last National Servicemen left the Armed Forces in May 1963.

Teenagers had come into their own in the 1950s; they had become a distinct group of people between childhood and adulthood. They had their very own fashions, music, and even language. But even in this there were variations.

There were different influences. One was the US motorcycle gangs: leathers, hard rock and roll and, of course, motorbikes. They looked back to the rock and roll years giving them the nickname 'Rockers'. Others looked more to Europe, with sharp Italian-style clothing, and Vespa or Lambretta motor scooters. This group were forward-looking, giving themselves the name 'Modernists', or just Mods.

In October 1962 the Beatles released their first UK single, 'Love Me Do', which peaked at number 17 in the charts. It was followed in January 1963 by 'Please Please Me', which reached number 1. That year they acquired the nickname 'the Fab Four', and the term 'Beatlemania' was coined to describe the scenes of wild frenzy that took place wherever the band appeared.

The Beatles brought new teenage fashions: the round-necked Beatle jacket, Cuban-heeled boots, high, tab-collared shirts, often in paisley, and the 'mop top' Beatle haircut. These innovations were seized upon by the Mods, for whom fashions were continually changing. Meanwhile, the Rockers' look changed very little: oily jeans, heavy boots, and a leather jacket over a long baggy jumper – ideal dress for motorcycling.

⋀ Beatlemania in Liverpool in 1964.

⋖ Mods on scooters in the 1960s.

The Mods and Rockers bank holiday riots in Brighton, 1964.

Flower children with painted bodies and faces during the 'love-in' at Woburn Abbey, 1967.

Differences in dress, outlook and even music developed from a harmless gulf to open hatred, and the Mods and Rockers would regularly clash, often with bloody results. These clashes reached the headlines in March 1964 when, during the long Easter weekend, thousands of them descended on the seaside town of Clacton. There followed a series of running battles between the two groups, to the horror of holidaymakers but to the delight of the press, amid calls for a return to National Service. Two months later was the Whitsun weekend, and Margate and Brighton saw the next clash of the Mods and Rockers.

By the second half of the decade things were changing again. The Mods were splitting: 'Peacock Mods' were dressing in ever-more outlandish clothes, such as the military-style coats seen on the 'Sergeant Pepper' LP cover, while the 'hard Mods' evolved into skinheads. The Peacock Mods turned into the 'hippies', staging 'love-ins' and festivals, where the Rockers, often wearing US-style Hell's Angels colours, acted as unofficial security. Yet whatever road 1960s teenagers took, it was most often a road of rebellion; as the Mod band The Who sang, 'Hope I die before I get old'.

In December 1961 Enoch Powell, then Minister of Health, announced that women who wished to use oral contraception ('the pill') would be able to get it on the National Health Service. One year later 50,000 were doing so, and by the end of the decade this had risen to one million, in spite of being condemned by the Catholic Church, among others, as a form of abortion.

The 1967 Abortion Act was introduced to Parliament as a free vote by the Liberal MP David Steel. This meant that parties would allow MPs to vote according to their conscience. It was passed in October, becoming law in April 1968. Abortion became legal on the British mainland at up to 28 weeks if two doctors agreed that the termination was in the mental and physical interests of the mother.

That same year Sheila Thorns gave birth by Caesarean section to sextuplets at Birmingham Maternity Hospital after undergoing fertility treatment. Sadly, three of the babies died. Fertility treatment was seen as a boon to childless couples, but many were put off by the possibility of multiple births.

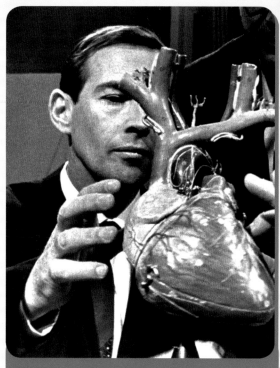

▲ Dr Christian Barnard, the South African surgeon, looks at a model of a human heart, 1967.

Large-scale immunisation against polio had begun in the late 1950s, causing the number of cases to drop dramatically; however, by 1961 there were still over 700 acute cases leading to 79 deaths in the UK. That year Albert Sabin pioneered an oral polio vaccine, and in 1962 Britain adopted it.

The 60s was the decade of transplants. The first UK kidney transplant was carried out at Edinburgh Royal Infirmary in October 1960. The operation was a great success, with both donor and recipient living for several more years. In November 1962 the first full hip replacement

◄ A thalidomide child, born without arms, at a party in London to mark the first anniversary of the Lady Hoare Thalidomide Appeal, 1963.

was carried out by Professor John Charnley at Wrightington Hospital, Wigan. Professor Charnley had spent years working on the problem, eventually pioneering his solution.

In December 1967 Christian Barnard carried out the first heart transplant operation in South Africa. Britain's first heart transplant took place at the National Heart Hospital in London, by Donald Ross, who led a team of 18 doctors and nurses. The patient survived the seven-hour procedure but died after 46 days from an infection.

In the United Kingdom the drug thalidomide had been licensed in 1958 and marketed as a cure for insomnia, coughs, colds and headaches. However,

doctors began to link it to birth defects in babies whose mothers had taken it while pregnant, and it was withdrawn in 1961. This was too late to prevent 2,000 babies being born with deformities in the UK. Of these, half died within a few months. The disaster led to far tighter and more stringent rules about the testing of new drugs.

Death rates were rising steeply from what were now being recognised as smoking-related causes. At the start of the 60s, around 70 per cent of men and 40 per cent of women in the UK smoked, but in 1962 the Royal College of Physicians issued a report which brought home to the public the long-term impact of smoking on health.

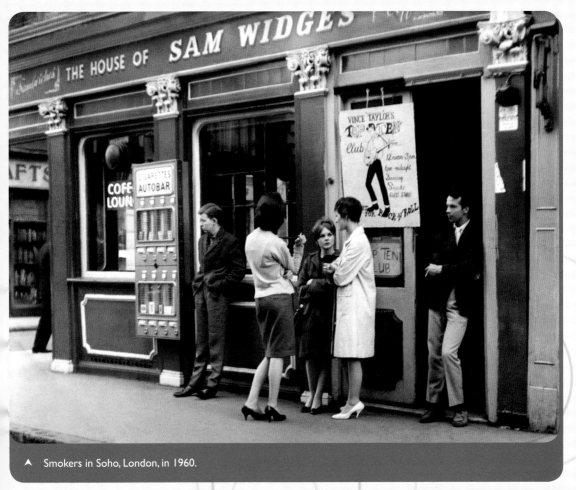

▲ Smokers in Soho, London, in 1960.

Fashion

Early 1960s fashions were casual: women would wear tight, ankle-length capri pants in pastel colours, with flat shoes and brightly coloured shirts or chunky sweaters, or a just-below-the-knee skirt or dress. Men would don fairly tight trousers (no turn ups), worn with a white shirt, sweater and a 'slim-jim' tie, or a sports jacket. Women generally wore their hair at shoulder-length, or in a bun or ponytail, while for men the fashion was a short Italian-style crop.

Changes came early. In 1964 bell-bottomed trousers began to replace capri pants. These were worn with a 60s classic polo-necked ribbed sweater, or alternatively with a chiffon blouse or short top which showed the midriff. That year, a young British designer called Mary Quant, who sold her designs from her clothes shop 'Bazaar' in London's Kings Road, created the miniskirt, which she named after the now-fashionable car. Also in 1964, André Courrèges launched his

▲ British fashion designer Mary Quant at work in London in 1963.

Space Age collection for women: trouser suits, geometric-shaped dresses and coats, helmets, boots and goggles, often all in white. His high boots, in white, became a trademark, especially when worn with a minidress or skirt.

The miniskirt, or minidress, grew ever shorter, and at its shortest became known as 'the pelmet'. It created a problem: stockings. Even quite modest minis showed off stocking tops and suspenders. Various solutions were sought – self-supporting stockings and very long socks among them – but the perfect remedy was nylon tights, which became hugely popular.

Other new man-made materials gave designers fresh opportunities. Crimplene, invented in the early 1950s, was much used in the 60s to make

◄ A white goatskin walking suit designed by André Courrèges of Paris, 1964.

▲ Carnaby Street, the 'Mod' fashion centre of London, 1967.

▲ Fashion by designer Mary Quant in London, 1967.

the typical A-line dress and, more shockingly, men's brightly coloured shirts. Whereas white had been almost compulsory, as the decade progressed pastel colours, then bright primaries, stripes and even paisley were acceptable, as was the new combination of a striped shirt with a white collar.

Women's hair, like their hemlines, was getting shorter. Vidal Sassoon invented the Nancy Kwan cut, a bob just below the jawline, and the shorter five-point bob, most famously worn by Mary Quant. The focus of the face was the eyes, which were heavily made up to appear as large as possible. On the other hand, men's hair was being worn ever longer, in a fashion made popular by the Beatles.

By the latter half of the 60s, Britain, and especially London, in the form of the Kings Road and Carnaby Street, had become the centre of world fashion. In 1966 the Nehru was the latest trend. This was a military-style coat, buttoning (often invisibly) all the way up to the throat, with a turned-up collar; it was named after the Indian Prime Minister. The jacket, like many designs

of the period, was unisex. Other short-lived fads included the paper dress, invented by the American Scott Paper Company in 1966, culottes, Afghan coats, and the crocheted minidress, which revealed a glimpse of underwear and in turn led to the see-through blouse and dress.

Popular Culture

The 'telly' had become the biggest form of mass entertainment; in 1960 over 11 million TV licences were issued, rising to more than 15 million by 1969. The two TV channels, BBC and ITV, were joined in 1964 by BBC2, which in 1967 broadcast the first colour programmes from Wimbledon. Two years later BBC and ITV began regular colour broadcasting.

Some of the highlights of 1960s TV included the start of *Coronation Street* in December 1960, the year when Nan Winton became the first female national newsreader on BBC. The following year, ITV's Westward, Border and Grampian regions were set up, while *The Avengers* and *Points of View* debuted. However, it was not until 1962 that ITV finally reached north-west Wales and the Channel Islands.

In August 1963 *Ready Steady Go* became the latest pop music programme, followed three months later by the first episode of *Doctor Who*. Entitled 'An Unearthly Child', it was broadcast in four weekly parts from 23 November to 14 December, starring William Hartnell as the

▲ Honor Blackman (Catherine Gale) and Patrick Mcnee (John Steed) of *The Avengers*, 1963.

Doctor, Carole Ann Ford as his granddaughter Susan, Jacqueline Hill as Barbara and William Russell as Chesterton.

In 1964 *Top of the Pops* and *Match of the Day* were both launched. But in 1965 came a notable 'last', as cigarette advertising was banned on television. Besides the iconic line from the World Cup finals – 'Some people are on the pitch – they think it's all over – it is now!' – 1966 also brought *Star Trek* and *Cathy Come Home*. In 1967 Patrick McGoohan was *The Prisoner* in a

The Rolling Stones in 1964.

Disc jockey Kenny Everett in 1969.

The Isle of Wight festival, 1969.

17-episode series which combined a spy story, science fiction, the surreal setting of Portmeirion, and often impenetrable plots, leaving viewers both confused and delighted. The following year, 1968, brought two huge favourites: *Dad's Army* and *The Morecombe and Wise Show*.

Music was evolving. In 1960 Chubby Checker introduced a new dance, 'the twist', and in 1963 the Rolling Stones released their first single, 'Come On'. It only reached number 21 in the charts, but in 1964 'It's All Over Now' reached number 1.

The outburst of 'pop' music left the BBC lagging behind; its output seemed very dated to the new generation. Illegal 'pirate' radio stations, broadcasting from offshore ships or disused sea forts, rose to prominence. The first was Radio Caroline, which started broadcasting from a ship off Essex in 1964, followed by 'Wonderful' Radio London. By 1967 21 pirate radio stations were broadcasting to an estimated daily audience of 10 to 15 million. The Government struck back using the Marine Broadcasting Offences Act of 1967, closing many down. They also restructured the BBC, establishing Radio 1, Radio 2, Radio 3 and Radio 4, using a number of ex-pirate DJs.

Pop music festivals became the latest thing. In 1968 the first Isle of Wight festival took place, followed a year later by the Woodstock festival in New York State.

▲ The new Austin Mini Countryman, an estate version of the Mini, 1960.

Car ownership was booming; in 1960 there were 5.7 million private and light goods vehicles licensed, rising to 8.9 million in 1965 and 11.2 million by 1970. New models included the Capri (1961), the Consul Cortina (1963) and the Ford Escort (1968).

The most iconic car of the decade was the Mini, designed by Sir Alec Issigonis and first produced in 1959. Issigonis had used a front-wheel-drive system and a transverse engine, which meant that the Mini was very small. This, and the front-wheel drive, made it extremely 'nippy', which, added to its low price and low fuel consumption, made it ideal for the younger generation. The Mini Cooper and Cooper 'S' were sportier versions, winning the Monte Carlo Rally every year from 1964 to 1967. There was also an estate version, a van and the Mini Moke. Produced between 1964 and 1968, Mini Mokes were variations on the US 'dune

buggy', favoured by surfers. Mini Mokes were never hugely popular and less than 15,000 were built.

At the other end of the scale was the E-type Jaguar, produced from 1961. With an engine four times the size of the Mini's, it could accelerate from 0 to 60mph in seven seconds and was one of the most beautiful cars ever made. The other iconic road vehicle was the motor scooter, and Vespas and Lambrettas in particular were popular with the Mods.

All this road traffic needed good roads. Britain's first full-length motorway, the M1, had opened between Watford and Crick in November 1959; between 1965 and 1968 it was extended from Crick to Leeds. In December 1965 a temporary 70mph speed limit was introduced, which was made permanent in 1967.

Better roads meant increasing competition with the railways. By 1965 rail passengers had fallen by 13 per cent from the previous decade. The war and

The 60s saw a huge rise in air travel, with the 10 million passengers passing through British terminals in 1960 virtually trebling to 28 million by 1969. The major airlines replaced their piston-engined aircraft with jets, such as Boeing 707s, DC8s and VC10s on long-haul routes, and Boeing 727s, Caravelles, BAC111s and Tridents on medium- and short-haul routes. For even shorter routes there were the new turbo-props. In 1969 the Anglo-French airliner Concorde made its first supersonic test flight.

△ Two Vespa scooters riding over Westminster Bridge, 1961.

△ M1 congestion in 1965.

the years following it had seen the rail network hugely underfunded. Much of it had become outdated and huge losses were being incurred. With the objective of stemming this, 1963 saw the publication of the first of two reports on Britain's railways by Dr Richard Beeching. It recommended 2,000 stations and 8,000 kilometres of line for closure, and a switch to containerisation for rail freight. These cuts became known as the Beeching Axe. In 1964 Japan launched its first 'Bullet Train', followed two years later by the first Inter-City trains in Britain.

The London Underground, however, had lost only 3 per cent of its passengers over the same period, and in 1962 construction began on the initial Walthamstow to Victoria section of the Victoria line, which opened in 1968.

➤ Chairman of the British Railways Board, Dr Richard Beeching, with a model of the modern Piccadilly Station, 1963.

Famous Faces

On a royal note, Prince Andrew, later Duke of York, the second son of the Queen and the Duke of Edinburgh, was born in February 1960 at Buckingham Palace. That same year his aunt, Princess Margaret, married photographer Antony Armstrong-Jones, who was created Earl of Snowdon in 1961. In March 1964 Prince Edward was born, now Earl of Wessex.

Photography was becoming respectable in the 1960s. In 1962 the Queen's cousin, Patrick Lichfield, began work as a photographer's assistant, and top photographers such as David Bailey and Terence Donovan became celebrities, as did their models. These included Lesley Hornby, better known as 'Twiggy', Jean Shrimpton 'the Shrimp', her sister Chrissie, US model Colleen Corby, and the German artist, actress and model Veruschka von Lehndorff. Clothes designers, such as Zandra Rhodes, Mary Quant, Ossie Clark and Barbara Hulanicki, were also part of 'the beautiful people'.

But the real celebrities of the 60s were the pop stars: some were famous for a few weeks; others, such as 'the Fab Four' and the Rolling Stones, became world famous as individuals. Some who had been stars in the 50s, such as Cliff Richard and, of course, Elvis Presley, remained at the top.

There were also sports celebrities, prominent among whom was the entire 1966 England World Cup squad, particularly Bobby Charlton, Bobby Moore and Nobby Styles. Other football celebrities included Jimmy Greaves and a young

◄ England's Martin Peters celebrates scoring his team's second goal during the 1966 World Cup Final.

George Best. Probably the biggest sporting star of the 60s was American heavyweight boxer Cassius Clay. He first rose to fame in the 1960 Rome Olympics, where he won the gold medal; then in 1964 he became world heavyweight boxing champion, beating Sonny Liston. Immediately afterwards he announced that he had become a Muslim and had changed his 'slave name' to Muhammad Ali. In 1967, with the Vietnam War raging, he refused to be drafted, stating that 'no Viet Cong ever called me nigger'. He was sentenced to five years in prison but was released on appeal. Another famous member of the 'Nation of Islam' was Malcolm Little, better known as Malcolm X. In 1965, shortly after repudiating the Nation of Islam, he was killed by three of its members.

It was a time of black militancy: in 1963, at the culmination of the March on Washington, Martin Luther King Jr delivered his 'I Have a Dream' speech; one year later in South Africa, Nelson Mandela, Walter Sisulu, Ahmed Kathrada

▲ Martin Luther King Jr acknowledging the crowd at the Lincoln Memorial for his 'I Have a Dream' speech, 1963.

and five others were sentenced to life in prison; and in 1966 Huey Newton and Bobby Seale formed the Black Panthers in the US.

The latter years of the decade seemed to be about death, as the newsreels showed endless film of Vietnam. In 1967 Che Guevara was killed; in 1968 both Martin Luther King Jr and Robert F. Kennedy were assassinated; and in 1969 the world was shocked by the Manson family murders. The family was part of an American quasi-commune, led by Charles Manson, who murdered seven people, including the actress Sharon Tate.

◄ American heavyweight Cassius Clay during a sparring session at the Drill Hall, London, 1963.

▲ An anti-Vietnam War protest, 1965.

➤ War Minister John Profumo resigns from the Government and as a Member of Parliament, 1963.

The 60s became the decade of protest. As a sign of things to come, in April 1960 at least 60,000 people gathered in Trafalgar Square at the end of the annual Aldermaston march in a protest against the H-bomb by the Campaign for Nuclear Disarmament.

Student activism played a great part in the protests of the period: in 1962 the first student protest against the Vietnam War was held in America; in 1965 a protest by 250 students occurred outside the American Consulate in Edinburgh, while another took place outside the embassy in Grosvenor Square, which a year later was the scene of a further demonstration by a crowd of over 4,000. Scuffles broke out between the police and protesters, and over 30 were arrested. All over the world, such protests became the norm: some were for local issues; many were anti-Vietnam War, anti-apartheid, or anti-racism. Some involved the sit-in or, in colleges, the teach-in, or the occupation of buildings. Another new phenomenon was the protest song, such as 'A Hard Rain's Gonna Fall' by Bob Dylan, or 'Eve of Destruction', sung by Barry McGuire.

In France, 1968 saw the closure of Paris University, Nanterre, because of friction between the students and the administration. In protest students at the Sorbonne began a demonstration, which escalated into a virtual insurrection by left-leaning groups.

In 1963 the 'Profumo scandal' broke, as the affair between Secretary of State for War John Profumo and Christine Keeler became public. The situation was made worse by the fact that she was also reputedly the mistress of a Soviet spy. When asked about it in the House of Commons, Profumo lied, and was eventually forced to resign.

Just a few months later, Prime Minister Harold Macmillan, 'Supermac', also resigned due to ill health, to be replaced by Sir Alec Douglas-Home. In the General Election, almost exactly one year later, Labour won with a slim majority of four seats, and Harold Wilson became the first Labour Prime Minister since 1951. And in 1966 Labour were re-elected with a much-increased majority of 98.

▲ Prime Minister Harold Macmillan with President John F. Kennedy, 1963.

In 1968 the Conservative MP Enoch Powell made a speech in Birmingham attacking the Government's immigration policy, calling for an immediate reduction in immigration and for the encouragement of immigrants in the UK to return home. He predicted racial strife: 'Like the Roman, I seem to see the river Tiber foaming with much blood.' It led to him being sacked from the shadow cabinet by party leader Ted Heath.

In 1969 the Representation of the People Act lowered the voting age in Britain to 18.

It was an era of independence: in 1961 Sierra Leone became independent, followed a year later by Jamaica, Trinidad and Tobago, Uganda, and Western Samoa. The year 1963 saw Kenya and Zanzibar given independence, followed in 1964 by Malawi and Malta, and in 1966 by Botswana, Gambia and Lesotho. However, things did not go smoothly for all nations. In 1961 South Africa left the Commonwealth due to its anti-apartheid stance, and in 1965 Rhodesia (now Zimbabwe) issued a Unilateral Declaration of Independence (UDI) in an effort to delay black majority rule.

◄ Christine Keeler, the model caught up in the Profumo Affair, 1963.

War & Peace

The Cold War was at its height. In February 1960 France exploded its first atomic weapon. In October 1961 the Soviet Union tested the 'Tsar Bomba'; it was the largest nuclear weapon ever tested.

The USA used high-flying U-2 'spy planes' against the Soviet Union, 'Red' China, North Vietnam and Cuba. In May 1960 a Soviet surface-to-air missile brought down a U-2 flown by Gary Powers over Russia. Powers was tried as a spy and sentenced to ten years in prison, but he was exchanged in 1962 for a captured Soviet agent.

In April 1961 a CIA-sponsored paramilitary invasion of Cuba was attempted. They landed in the Bay of Pigs, overwhelming local militias, but within three days they were rounded up and sent back to the USA, leaving behind over 100 dead.

In August that same year the construction of the Berlin Wall began; it was an attempt to prevent the exodus of East Berliners to the West. Crossing the wall continued, however, and in 1962 the first person was killed while trying to reach West Berlin.

In May 1962 Nikita Khrushchev and Fidel Castro agreed to place Soviet nuclear missiles in Cuba to deter another invasion attempt, and in October nuclear missiles were photographed on the island. In response, the USA blockaded Cuba in order to halt the delivery of further Soviet weapons. Khrushchev called it 'an act of aggression propelling human kind into the abyss of a world nuclear-missile war'. Behind-the-scenes negotiations began, but while they were taking place, Soviet ships tried to run the blockade and US ships were ordered to open fire if necessary. On 28 October an agreement was reached; Russian missiles were withdrawn, as were US missiles in Turkey and Italy. Meanwhile, America agreed never to invade Cuba.

For two weeks the world had stared nuclear destruction in the face; to try to avoid a

The construction of the Berlin Wall, 1961.

> Soviet Premier Nikita Khrushchev (right) toasts the signing of the Limited Test Ban Treaty, 1963.

◄ Cuban leader Fidel Castro (centre) during the negotiations to release people captured during the Bay of Pigs invasion in 1961.

repetition, in 1963 a 'hotline' was set up between the US and the USSR. That same year the Soviet Union, America, the UK and many non-nuclear states signed the Limited Test Ban Treaty, banning nuclear tests either underwater, in the atmosphere or in outer space. Underground testing was permitted, however. In 1964 China became the fifth nuclear power; two years later China tested its first hydrogen bomb.

In March 1965, in an attempt to prevent a Communist takeover of South Vietnam by the North Vietnamese Army and the Viet Cong, the US airforce began the large-scale bombing of North Vietnam, while US troop numbers increased from 75,000 to 200,000. In 1968 the Viet Cong launched the Tet Offensive, attacking targets throughout the south. The attack failed, but it shook both the US administration and the public. Public opinion was further turned against the war by news of the My Lai Massacre of Vietnamese villagers by US troops in 1968.

The Palestinian Liberation Organization was formed in 1964. In June 1967 Israel launched a pre-emptive attack, destroying the Egyptian, Jordanian, Syrian and Iraqi air forces. In what became known as the Six Day War, Israel gained the Sinai Peninsula, Gaza Strip, West Bank, east Jerusalem and the Golan Heights.

◄ Israeli soldiers dance in celebration at the Wailing Wall in Old Jerusalem after removing the city from Arab control in 1967.

Tottenham Hotspur became the first club in the 20th century to achieve the League and FA Cup double in the 1960/61 season. They won the FA Cup again in 1962, and in 1963 became the first British club to win the European Cup Winners' Cup.

In 1960 Penguin published the unexpurgated edition of *Lady Chatterley's Lover* and was taken to court under the Obscene Publications Act. The Act allowed publication if a work was of literary merit. Many experts testified, and the trial became a test of how permissive society was becoming. One memorable incident occurred when the prosecutor asked the jury: 'Is it a book you would even wish your wife or your servants to read?' The verdict of 'not guilty' split Britain, with some conservative elements going on to form the National Viewers' and Listeners' Association; their most famous member was Mary Whitehouse.

In August 1963 a Royal Mail train was targeted by thieves in what became known as the Great Train Robbery. A gang of 15, including Bruce Reynolds, Buster Edwards and Ronnie Biggs, stole over £2.6 million after coshing the train driver with a metal bar. Within weeks, 11 of the gang were arrested, and in 1964 nine of these, including Biggs, were given long sentences.

▲ After being banned for over 30 years, D.H. Lawrence's book, *Lady Chatterley's Lover*, sells out hours after being released, 1960.

Reynolds and Edwards escaped to Mexico, but Edwards returned to England in 1966 and was given 15 years. Reynolds spent five years on the run before being sentenced to 25 years in 1969. Ronnie Biggs served 15 months before escaping from prison in 1965; he managed to remain free for 36 years and died in 2013.

Britain's last hanging took place in 1964 when Peter Allen and Gwynn Evans were executed for the murder of John West. The following year Parliament voted to suspend capital punishment for a five-year trial period, after which it was abolished.

In 1966 the Post Office Tower was officially opened by Tony Benn and Billy Butlin. At a height of 626 feet, it was then Britain's tallest building. Its special feature was the revolving restaurant at

◄ Ronald Biggs is sentenced to 30 years in prison for his role in the Great Train Robbery, 1964.

The Duke of Edinburgh is surrounded by rescue workers as he picks his way through the sludge in front of the wrecked school at Aberfan, South Wales, 1966.

The Post Office Tower near Tottenham Court Road in London, 1964.

the top, which was operated by Butlin's. That July the eighth FIFA World Cup was held in England. The England team under Bobby Moore beat West Germany 4–2 in the final, with Geoff Hurst scoring a hat-trick.

The country was shocked in October 1966 by the Aberfan disaster, when a colliery spoil heap collapsed, burying nearby homes and a school. In all, 116 children and 28 adults were killed.

December 1968 saw Britain deeply shocked by the case of Mary Bell, an 11-year-old on trial at Newcastle Assizes for having strangled first 4-year-old Martin Brown, and two months later, 3-year-old Brian Howe. The case was doubly troubling because no reasons for the murders could be established. Bell was found guilty of manslaughter due to diminished responsibility, a verdict which split opinion between those who saw her as a deeply troubled child needing treatment, and those who saw her as evil incarnate and the whole case as an example of the damage being done to society's moral fabric by liberal attitudes.

In April 1960 the capital of Brazil was moved from Rio de Janeiro to a brand new city, Brasilia. One month later the most powerful earthquake ever recorded hit Chile. Rating 9.5 on the Richter scale, the earthquake, and the subsequent tsunami, affected Hawaii, Japan, the Philippines, New Zealand, Australia and the Aleutian Islands, leaving at least 2,000 dead.

In North America, 1960 saw the first televised presidential debates between Vice President Richard Nixon and John F. Kennedy. Nixon was generally considered to have come over the best by those listening to the radio, but on TV Kennedy looked more attractive, and was elected in November.

The USSR continued to lead America in the Space Race and Yuri Gagarin became the first human in outer space when his Vostok spacecraft orbited the earth in April 1961. One month later, Alan Shepard became the first American in space. That month, the new US President set a goal, 'before this decade is out, of landing a man on the moon and returning him safely to the earth'. It was a goal he would never see fulfilled as, just over 18 months later, he was assassinated in Dallas. His death created a host of conspiracy theories, which were not calmed by the publication, in 1964, of the Warren Report.

˄ Survivors clean up debris of a building in Concepcion, Chile, in 1960, which was destroyed during an earthquake.

˂ Flowers are placed near the site where President John F. Kennedy was assassinated, 1963.

Astronaut Edwin E. Aldrin Jr walks on the surface of the moon, 30 July 1969.

Lincoln Memorial. The following year the Civil Rights Act was passed. In October 1964 King received the Nobel Peace Prize. Then in April 1968 he was assassinated in Memphis, Tennessee, by James Earl Ray.

Six months later, at the Olympics in Mexico, two black US athletes, Tommie Smith and John Carlos, who had been first and third in the 200-metre final, gave a clenched-fist salute from the podium as 'The Star-Spangled Banner' was played; they were expelled from the Games and had their medals taken away.

The USSR continued to vie for supremacy and in June 1963 Valentina Tereshkova became the first woman in space. But, by July 1969 the USA had taken the lead, and Apollo 11 became the first manned mission to land on the moon.

People could now watch events on TV as they happened, thanks to great advances in broadcasting. The 1964 Summer Olympics in Tokyo was the first to be telecast internationally using the first geostationary communication satellite. It was also the first Olympics from which South Africa was barred, due to its apartheid system in sports. The spotlight had been on the country since international outrage had broken out over the Sharpeville massacre, which had occurred in March 1960 at a police station; a crowd of around 6,000 demonstrators had been fired upon by police, leaving 69 dead.

In the USA, also, segregation was being challenged. In 1961 the 'Freedom Riders' protested against continuing segregation on interstate buses, and in August 1963 250,000 people took part in the March on Washington, at the end of which Martin Luther King Jr delivered his 'I Have a Dream' speech from the steps of the

Extending gloved hands skyward in racial protest, US athletes Tommie Smith (centre) and John Carlos stare downward during the playing of 'The Star Spangled Banner', 1968.

Important Dates

1960

In July Francis Chichester sails *Gipsy Moth II* into New York Harbour, becoming the first solo Atlantic yachtsman.

1961

In December 'the pill' is prescribed for the first time, to married women.

1962

In October the Beatles release their first single and appear on television for the first time.

1963

In August a gang rob the London to Glasgow Royal Mail train in what would become known as the Great Train Robbery.

1964

Violent clashes between the Mods and Rockers break out in Clacton-on-Sea over the Easter bank holiday; and again in Brighton at Whitsun.

1965

In October Ian Brady is arrested on suspicion of murder, followed a few days later by his girlfriend, Myra Hindley.

1966

England win the football World Cup; in March the cup itself had been stolen while on show at Westminster, only to be found by a dog, Pickles, in Norwood, south London.

1967

In July the first colour television broadcasts begin with the Wimbledon Championships.

1968

In November the Race Relations Act is passed, making it illegal to discriminate on the grounds of ethnic background in terms of housing, employment or public services.

1969

In January the Beatles give their last public performance, an impromptu affair on the roof of the Apple Records building, which is stopped by the police.

Acknowledgements

Written by Mike Brown. The author has asserted his moral rights.
Edited by Abbie Wood.
Designed by Jemma Cox.

All photographs have been supplied by PA Images.

Every effort has been made to contact the copyright holders; the publisher will be pleased to rectify any omissions in future editions.

Text © Pitkin Publishing.

Publication in this form © Pitkin Publishing 2014.

Printed in Great Britain.

ISBN 978-1-84165-540-6   1/14